Professor Pete's Prehistoric Animals

HORNED
DINOSAURS

W
FRANKLIN WATTS
LONDON • SYDNEY

Franklin Watts
This edition published in the UK in 2017 by The Watts Publishing Group

Copyright © 2013 David West Children's Books

Designed and illustrated by David West

ISBN 978 1 4451 5506 7

Printed in Malaysia

Franklin Watts
An imprint of
Hachette Children's Group
Part of The Watts Publishing Group
Carmelite House
50 Victoria Embankment
London EC4Y 0DZ

An Hachette UK Company.
www.hachette.co.uk

www.franklinwatts.co.uk

PROFESSOR PETE'S PREHISTORIC ANIMALS HORNED DINOSAURS
was produced for Franklin Watts by
David West Children's Books, 6 Princeton Court, 55 Felsham Road, London SW15 1AZ

Professor Pete says:
This little guy will tell you something more about the animal.

Learn what this animal ate.

Where and when (Mya=Millions of Years Ago) did it live?

Its size is revealed!

How fast or slow was it?

Discover the meaning of its name.

A timeline on page 24 shows you the dates of the different periods in Mya.

Contents

Archaeoceratops 4

Diabloceratops 6

Einiosaurus 8

Pachyrhinosaurus 10

Pentaceratops 12

Protoceratops 14

Styracosaurus 16

Torosaurus 18

Triceratops 20

Zuniceratops 22

Glossary and Timeline 24

Archaeoceratops

ahr-kee-oh-serra-tops

Archaeoceratops was a very old member of the horned dinosaur family. It didn't have horns but it did have a small bony **frill** extending from the back of its head.

Archaeoceratops means 'ancient horned face'.

Archaeoceratops was quite speedy for a horned dinosaur.

Archaeoceratops was about 0.9 metres long and weighed around 2.3–4.5 kilogrammes.

It lived in China during the Lower Cretaceous period, 125–115 Mya.

Archaeoceratops was a plant eater. It ate ferns, **cycads** and conifers.

Professor Pete says:
This little dinosaur ran about on two legs which is unusual for the horned dinosaurs. Most of them walked on all fours.

Diabloceratops

dee-AB-loh-serra-tops

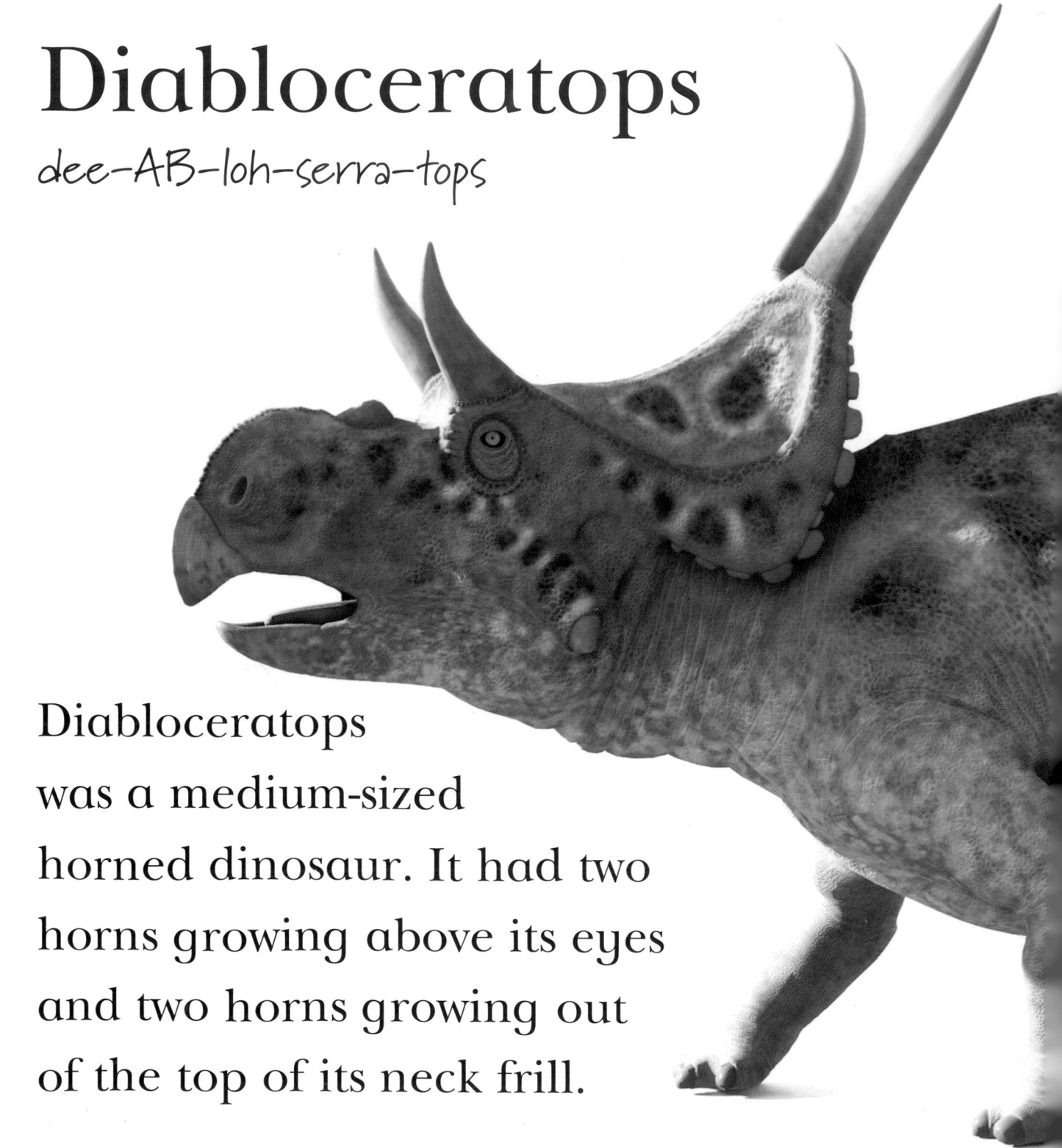

Diabloceratops
was a medium-sized
horned dinosaur. It had two
horns growing above its eyes
and two horns growing out
of the top of its neck frill.

Diabloceratops was a plant eater.

Diabloceratops was similar to a modern-day rhino and could probably run up to 40.2 kilometres per hour.

It lived in the United States during the Upper Cretaceous period, 85 Mya.

Diabloceratops means 'devil horned face'.

Diabloceratops grew up to 6 metres in length and weighed 3.6 tonnes.

Professor Pete says:
Like all the horned dinosaurs, Diabloceratops had a beak. It used it to rip away tough plant material from trees and cycads.

7

Einiosaurus

ie-nee-oh-sore-us

The first thing you notice about this dinosaur is the strange curved horn on its nose. It might have been used in defence against **predators**.

Professor Pete says:
These horned dinosaurs roamed the plains of North America in herds, like buffalo do today.

8

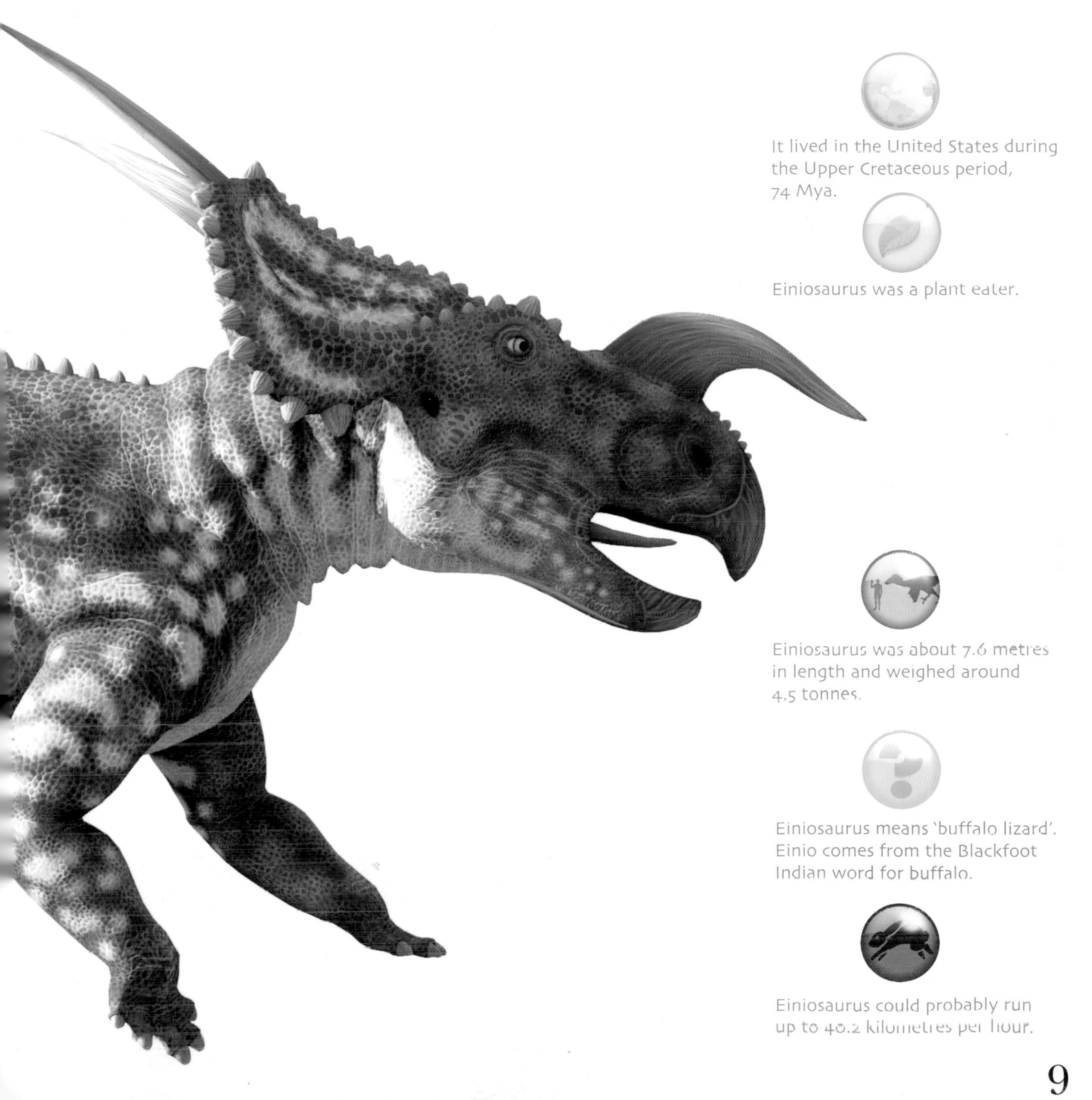

It lived in the United States during the Upper Cretaceous period, 74 Mya.

Einiosaurus was a plant eater.

Einiosaurus was about 7.6 metres in length and weighed around 4.5 tonnes.

Einiosaurus means 'buffalo lizard'. Einio comes from the Blackfoot Indian word for buffalo.

Einiosaurus could probably run up to 40.2 kilometres per hour.

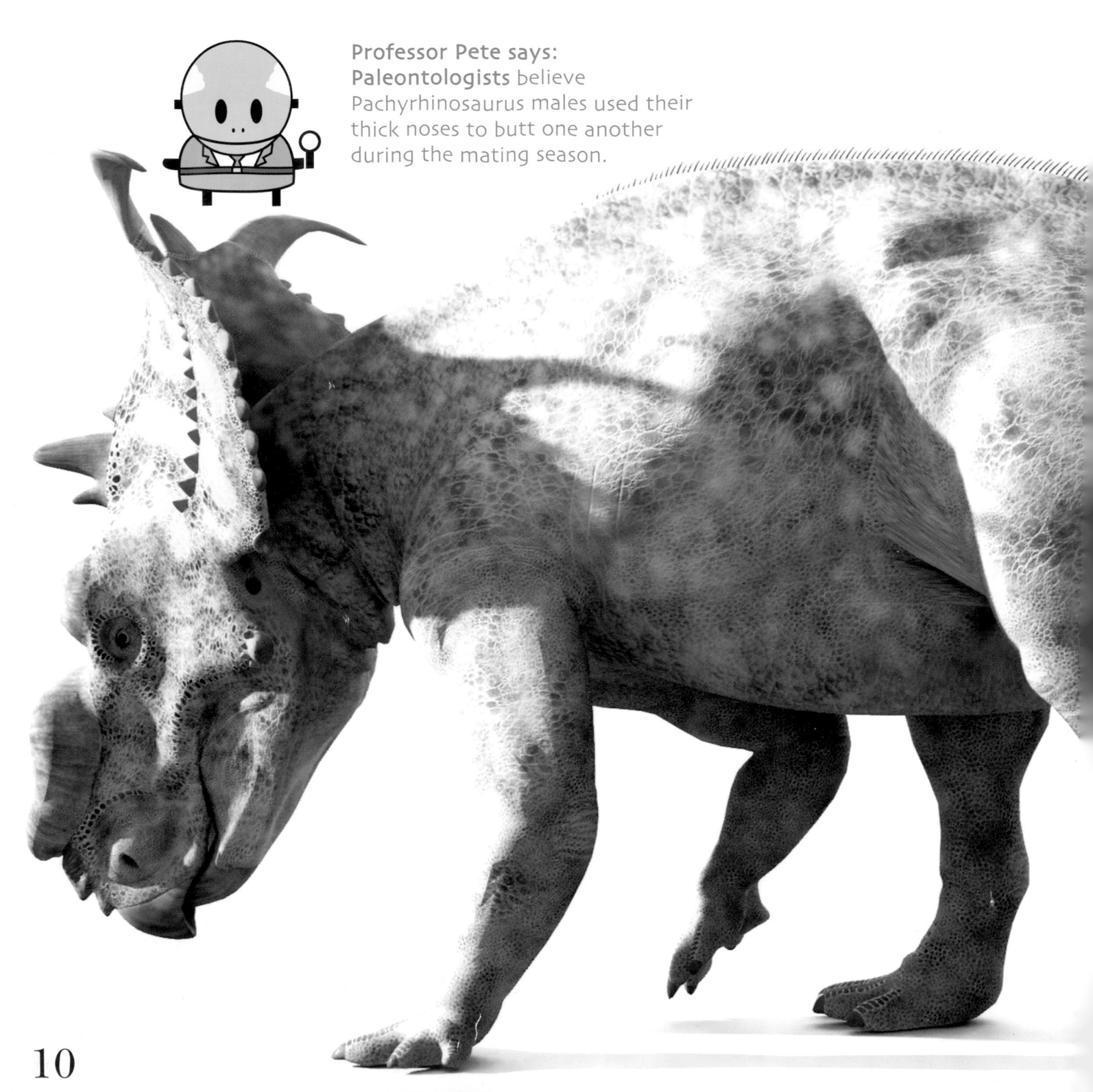

Professor Pete says:
Paleontologists believe
Pachyrhinosaurus males used their
thick noses to butt one another
during the mating season.

10

 Pachyrhinosaurus was a plant eater.

 Pachyrhinosaurus means 'thick-nosed lizard'.

 It lived in Canada during the Upper Cretaceous period, 76–74 Mya.

 Pachyrhinosaurus was very nimble. It probably reached speeds of 32.2 kilometres per hour.

 Pachyrhinosaurus grew up to 6 metres in length and weighed 3.6 tonnes.

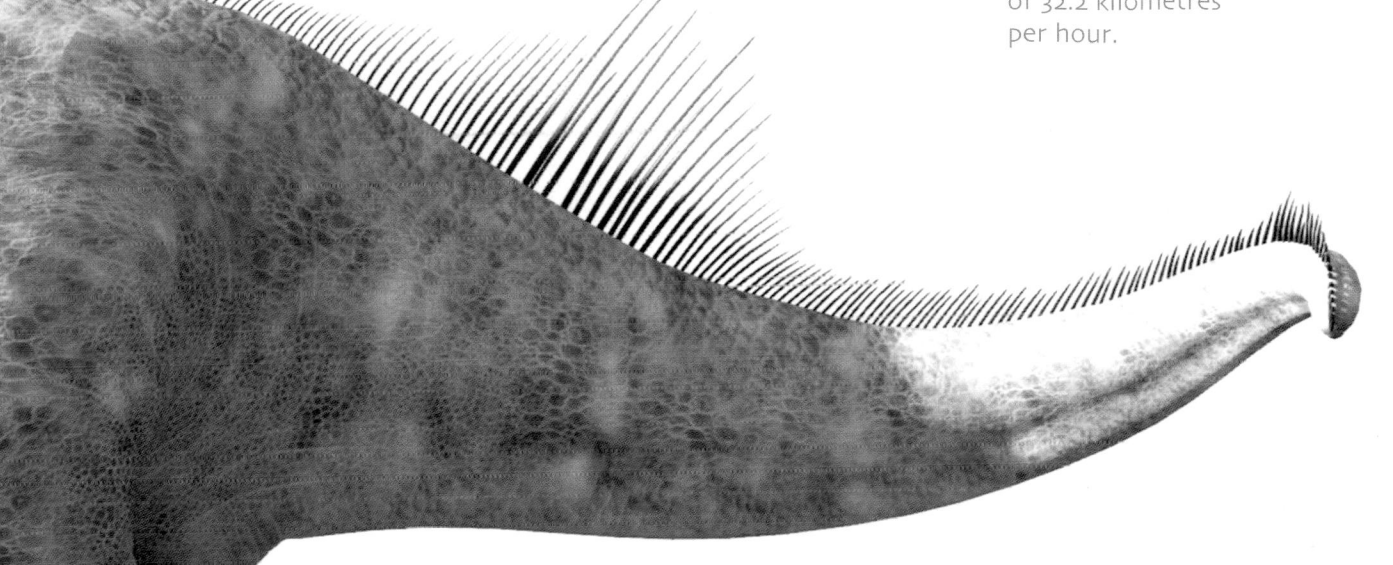

Pachyrhinosaurus

pack-ee-RINE-oh-sore-us

This horned dinosaur had a flattened area of bone above its eyes and nose instead of horns.

11

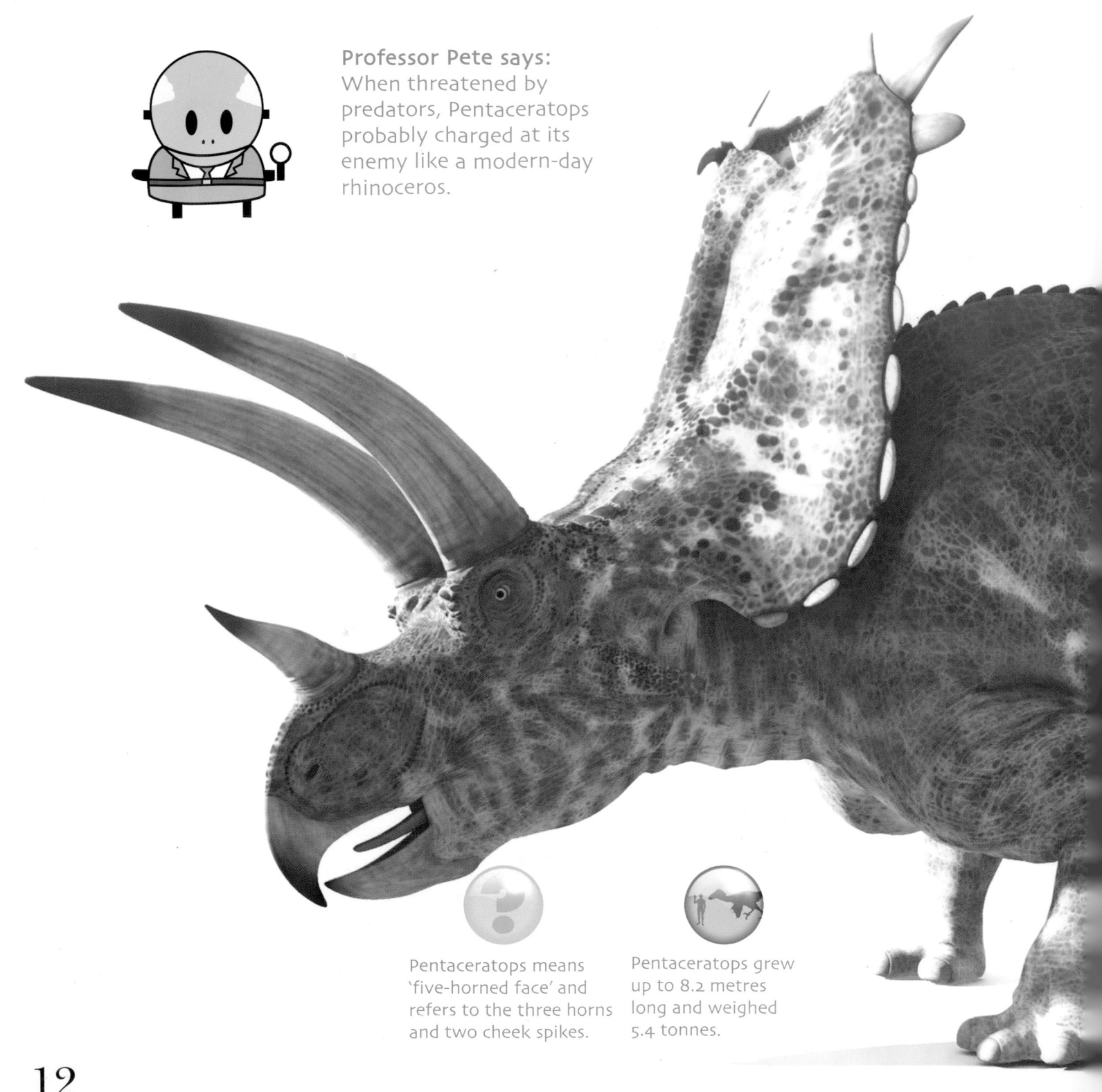

Professor Pete says:
When threatened by predators, Pentaceratops probably charged at its enemy like a modern-day rhinoceros.

Pentaceratops means 'five-horned face' and refers to the three horns and two cheek spikes.

Pentaceratops grew up to 8.2 metres long and weighed 5.4 tonnes.

Pentaceratops

pent-ah-ker-ah-tops

From the tip of its beak to the top of its bony frill, Pentaceratops had one of the largest heads of any dinosaur. Its frill was probably coloured to attract female Pentaceratops.

Pentaceratops was a plant eater, eating ferns, cycads and conifers.

Pentaceratops probably reached speeds of 32.2 kilometres per hour.

It lived in the United States during the Upper Cretaceous period, 76–74 Mya.

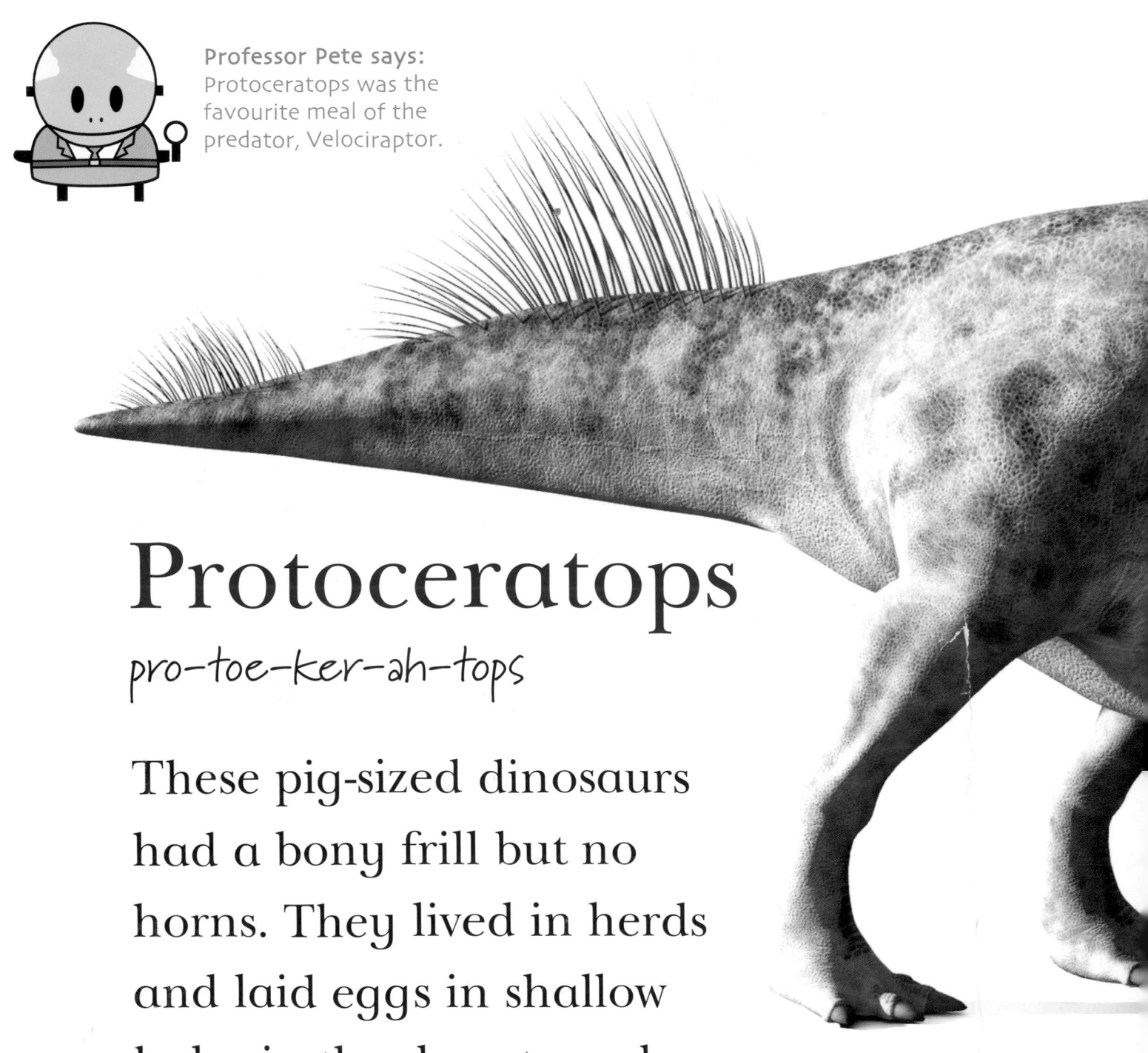

Protoceratops

pro-toe-ker-ah-tops

These pig-sized dinosaurs had a bony frill but no horns. They lived in herds and laid eggs in shallow holes in the desert sand.

 Protoceratops was a plant eater.

 Protoceratops could run as fast as a pig; 24.1 kilometres per hour.

 It lived in Mongolia during the Upper Cretaceous period, 85–80 Mya.

 Protoceratops means 'first horned face'.

 Protoceratops grew up to 1.6 metres in length and weighed around 181 kilogrammes.

15

Styracosaurus

sty-RAK-oh-sore-us

This spiky dinosaur had six large horns sticking out from the edge of its frill. It also had a huge nose horn which grew up to 61 centimetres long.

 Styracosaurus was a plant eater. It ate cycads, palms and other plants with its beak.

 Styracosaurus was relatively fast and could probably run at 32.2 kilometres per hour.

 It lived in Canada and the United States during the Upper Cretaceous period, 76–70 Mya.

 Styracosaurus means 'spiked lizard'.

 Styracosaurus grew up to 5.5 metres long and weighed 2.7 tonnes.

Professor Pete says:
Its frightening array of horns may have been a means of defence, either to **gore** hungry raptors and tyrannosaurs or to make itself look larger and more threatening.

Torosaurus

TOR-oh-sore-us

This dinosaur's frilled skull measured a massive 2.6 metres in length. It had two large horns that

made good defensive weapons.

Professor Pete says:
The huge bony frill had two large holes in it to make it lighter. The skin growing over the frill covered these holes.

 Torosaurus was a plant eater.

 Torosaurus means 'perforated lizard' after the holes in its frill.

 It lived in Canada and the United States during the Upper Cretaceous period, 70–65 Mya.

 Torosaurus was the size of an elephant. It could probably run 40.2 kilometres per hour.

 Torosaurus grew up to 7.6 metres in length and weighed 6 tonnes.

19

Triceratops

tri-SERRA-tops

The frill and horn were used mainly in **courtship**. Scratch marks on a Triceratops's skull suggest it had fought another Triceratops.

 Triceratops ate plants.

 Triceratops means 'three-horned face'.

 Triceratops was 9.1 metres long and 11.8 tonnes in weight.

 Triceratops was a fast heavy-weight and could probably run 32.1 kilometres per hour over a short distance.

 It lived in the United States during the Upper Cretaceous period, 67–65 Mya.

Professor Pete says: Triceratops had good eyesight, hearing and sense of smell to help keep it out of danger.

 Zuniceratops ate plants.

 Zuniceratops lived in the United States during the Upper Cretaceous period, 44–89 Mya.

 Zuniceratops means 'Zuni-horned face' after the Zuni tribe, natives of New Mexico.

 Zuniceratops was a lightweight and might have had a top speed of 32.1 kilometres per hour.

 It measured up to 3.4 metres long, and weighed up to 114 kilogrammmes.

Professor Pete says:
The fossils of Zuniceratops were found in New Mexico in the United States by an eight-year-old boy.

22

Zuniceratops
ZOO-nee-serra-tops

This small horned
dinosaur had two
upwards curving
eyebrow horns.

Glossary

courtship
The behaviour of animals aimed at attracting a mate.

cycads
Palm-like plants.

frill
Bony plate that curves up behind the skull.

gore
Pierce or wound with something pointed.

paleontologist
A scientist who studies early forms of life.

predators
Animals that hunt and eat other animals.

Timeline

Dinosaurs lived during the Mesozoic Era which is divided into three main periods.

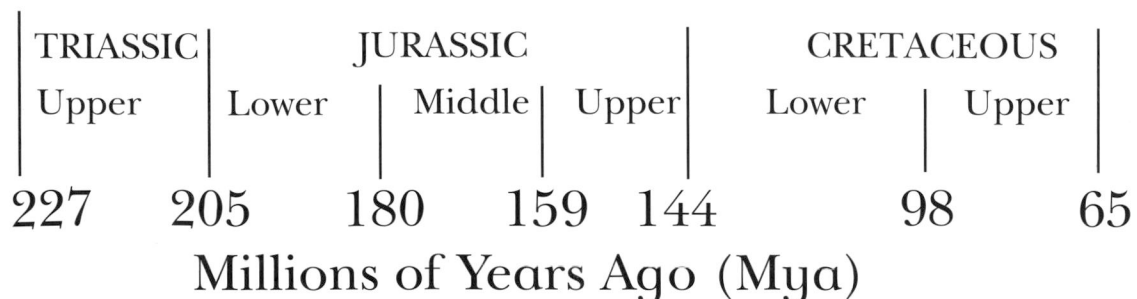

TRIASSIC		JURASSIC			CRETACEOUS	
Upper	Lower	Middle	Upper	Lower	Upper
227	205	180	159	144	98	65

Millions of Years Ago (Mya)